AUDITIONING

What to choose, where to find it and how to prepare it

A Practical Guide for the Would-be Actor and Drama Student

BY

RONA LAURIE

B.A. (Hons.), F.G.S.M., L.R.A.M., G.O.D.A.

Professor of Speech, Drama and Public Speaking, Guildhall School of Music and Drama

J. GARNET MILLER LTD

TO MY STUDENTS

IN GRATITUDE

FOR ALL THAT THEY HAVE TAUGHT ME

First published in 1985 by
J. Garnet Miller Ltd
311 Worcester Road, Malvern, Worcestershire

2nd impression, 1989

ISBN 0 85343 585 5

Typeset by Katerprint Co. Ltd, Oxford

Printed in Great Britain by BPCC Wheatons Ltd, Exeter

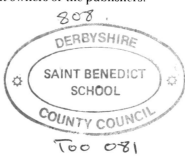

CONTENTS

Page

INTRODUCTION, AUDITION SPEECHES 7

AN ACTOR'S LIFE FOR YOU? 9

ADVICE ON AUDITIONS AND PREPARATION... 11

'AS YOU LIKE IT' 15

'TABLE MANNERS' 17

SUGGESTIONS FOR AUDITION SPEECHES........ 20

SPEECHES (TABULATED) 21

SUMMARY 64

Audition Speeches

(What to choose and Where to find it)

THIS book is designed to meet two specific needs. First it is planned to help would-be actors who have applied for auditions at Drama Schools, and secondly to be of use to drama students who are already being trained and are now looking for suitable material to have in their repertoire when they go into the profession.

I have been aware during the past few years of the ever-increasing number of applicants for stage training (the Television series "Fame" has a lot to answer for!) and of the fact that the number of places available at Drama Schools has not, like-wise, increased. Inevitably much frustration and heartbreak has been experienced by the vast majority of young people who fail to win one of the coveted places. Often the actual audition has had a shattering effect on them, regardless of the result. A bored panel of judges can produce as devastating an effect as a tough one.

And yet much of the distress caused by failure to be offered a place, or even a recall for further consideration could be avoided, or at least mitigated, by the careful selection and preparation of material. The audition may be turned into a worth-while experience, whatever the result.

Finding the right speech involves a good deal of time and research. Therefore I have made a list of suggestions for audition speeches, covering a wide range of moods, styles and ages.

Once the would-be actor has been accepted by a Drama School the search for good audition material still goes on. And so in addition to the list of material suggested for auditions to Drama Schools, there is a list of suggested speeches for drama students.

I hope that this book will prove useful to both the would-be actor and to the trained student about to enter the profession.

RONA LAURIE

An actor's life for you?

"The profession is overcrowded
And the struggle's pretty tough
And admitting the fact
She's burning to act,
That isn't quite enough."
(NOEL COWARD)

EVERY YEAR thousands apply to drama schools for auditions. Of these thousands a very small percentage indeed is admitted. Many applicants are not aware of the fierce competition for places and it might be a salutary exercise if they managed to get hold of the statistics from the leading drama schools indicating how many applied for places each year and how many were accepted. The information could then be printed on a large poster which could be hung on the back of the bedroom door as a reminder of the odds involved.

However, the person who wants to get into the theatre is unlikely to be put off by statistics, no matter how daunting. Discouragement has probably already been given by friends, relations, teachers and by those already in the profession. The latter are usually the most vociferous in their warnings against choosing the stage as a career. Despite what some cynics have suggested, these warnings are not prompted by the selfish instinct of the actor to ward off any possible future competition; they are given because actors know, only too well, the hazards, frustration and heartache which are likely to be experienced by anyone entering their overcrowded profession.

To get a realistic picture of the current position regarding work in the theatre, the aspiring drama student could add to that poster on the bedroom door Equity's latest figures for how many of its members were out of work.

Leaving statistics aside for the moment, why is it that people so often discourage anyone who says that he wants to act professionally?

There are a number of reasons. It may be because clear-sighted friends and relations think that the necessary talent is lacking; or teachers may take a realistic view of the chances of a youngster making a living in the theatre.

Parents' attitudes are unpredictable. But in many cases their reaction is one of horror when the school-leaver suddenly announces at the breakfast table "I want to be an actor".

All this discouragement and well-meant advice usually falls on deaf ears, because few people are so determined and tenacious as those who want to go on the stage. This tenacity is, of course, one of the necessary attributes of the actor but it can also lead to a failure to accept facts and to consequent disappointment and frustration.

Therefore in view of the competition to get into a drama school and the subsequent competition which awaits the trained drama student, would-be actors should ask themselves certain questions before even applying for an audition.

9

Have I any talent?

They usually answer "Yes" to this first question. This conviction may or may not be justified. It is, of course, possible that there is talent there. On the other hand it may be that he or she has been overpraised for a performance in a school play. A well-directed child can sometimes create a strong impression, but few schoolboy Katharines are potential Oliviers even if they have made a success in the part. A false idea has been given of the child's acting ability. Or it may be that a child has done well in the drama section of a Music Festival and an adjudicator has been indiscreet enough to say "You ought to go into the theatre".

Then, too, parents often give their offspring an inflated view of their gifts as an actor. Sometimes they may be pressurised into a stage career in order to fulfill the thwarted ambition of one parent or another ("*What a good idea to go to drama school! When I was young I always wanted to be an actor.*")

All these factors should be borne in mind before the question "Have I any talent?" is answered.

Would I be miserable doing anything else but acting?

The answer to this should, of course, be "Yes". However, many people who are insufficiently motivated try to get into a drama school. Some of these actually succeed in winning one of the much-coveted places. I once asked a conspicuously un-talented student what had made him want to go into the theatre. "Oh, I thought I'd give it a whirl" was the reply. Collapse of the rest of the class!

Some apply for auditions merely because they are bored with the job they are in.

Am I dazzled by the glamour of the stage?

If the answer to this is "Yes", it would be a good idea to ask someone who has toured extensively, or has been in a struggling repertory company, or who has had to endure long periods out of work (euphemistically known as 'resting') what life in the theatre can be like.

And yet the stage undoubtedly has glamour and always will have, so this is a tricky question to answer honestly. I suppose the operative word is 'dazzled'. Be sure that the other side of the picture is also realised—the hard work, the often uncomfortable, even squalid working conditions and, above all, the precariousness of the profession.

Advice on choice of audition speeches and their preparation

"In all theatrical experience I know of nothing more dispiriting than an average audition." (NOEL COWARD)

So you have decided to apply to one or two drama schools for an audition. How should you set about preparing your material?

Is it wise to have coaching?

Some drama schools advise you against going to a drama coach or teacher for help in the choice and preparation of audition speeches.

However in my experience I find that most of the successful applicants have received some form of coaching or training. But obviously you should be very careful in the choice of coach. Bad advice and training are worse than none at all and may result in the kind of drilled, artificial performance that is anathema to those who are judging you.

Go to someone experienced, of proved ability, preferably to someone with a professional stage background and who is actively concerned in the theatre.

A good coach will advise you as to choice of material and many pitfalls will be avoided at the outset.

Even professional actors don't always know what suits them best and this applies still more to the inexperienced student.

The technique of auditions

Always make sure that you know the length of the speech that is stipulated by each drama school. These times vary but are usually not longer than two or three minutes. It is wise to choose speeches that are slightly under time. Panels on audition days are working to a very tight schedule and it would be a pity to be cut off just as you were working up to the climax of your performance.

Find out how many speeches are called for, and, if set speeches are given, how many of them have to be learned by heart. Your 'own choice' speeches should always be memorised.

It is surprising how many turn up for auditions not even knowing their lines.

What not to choose

Possibly the most helpful advice I can give at this stage concerns what *not* to choose. So many people ruin any chance of success that they might have by an unwise choice.

11

1. Avoid very well-known speeches; 'purple passages' from Shakespeare, for example, however drawn to them you might be: "To be or not to be", "All the world's a stage" and "The quality of mercy is not strain'd" for instance. All I can say is that it certainly will be strained among the judges, who have had to sit through these 'golden oldies' time and time again. I am sure that those of us who sit on panels could draw up lists of speeches which we hope never to hear again. In fact RADA has issued the following list under the heading *Speeches not to be performed for Audition*:

FEMALE
Viola from 'Twelfth Night': 'I left no ring with her.'
Phebe from 'As You Like It': 'Think not I love him though I ask for him.'
Ophelia from 'Hamlet': ALL her speeches.
Helena from 'A Midsummer Night's Dream': 'How happy some o'er other some can be!'
Rosalind from 'As You Like It':The Epilogue.
Kate from 'The Taming of the Shrew': Her final speech.
Julia from 'The Two Gentlemen of Verona': 'Nay, would I were so ang'red with the same.'

MALE
Mercutio from 'Romeo and Juliet': 'Oh then I see Queen Mab hath been with you.'
Malvolio from 'Twelfth Night': Act II scene 5.
Launcelot Gobbo from 'The Merchant of Venice': 'Certainly my conscience will serve me to run from this Jew, my master.'
Launce from 'The Two Gentlemen of Verona': 'Nay, 'twill be this hour ere I have done weeping.'

2. Don't over-assess your present acting ability by choosing a speech that is much too difficult for you. Speeches of such technical difficulty that they would test the skill of even the most experienced professional are often chosen.

3. Don't choose a character for whom you are physically completely unsuited. You should always take your physical attributes into account. Few of us are able to be realistic about what we really look like, but when choosing material to perform, one's appearance should always be borne in mind. For example, avoid the characters of Rosalind and Helena if you are very short. And you may think that you will be a wow as Cleopatra, but unless you have considerable physical allure, you are unlikely to be successful in the part.

4. Don't choose two speeches which are in the same mood, or which are written in exactly the same style. It is much better to show a range and this gives you more chance of success. You may act one of the speeches badly, but the other one, the contrasted one, so well that you are able to give a true picture of your potential. You will not have put all your eggs in one basket.

5. Don't make a choice into which you have been pressurised by someone else and in which you feel ill at ease and insecure.

6. Don't choose a comedy speech unless you are well aware of the difficulty of bringing it off successfully under the audition conditions, in front of a panel of judges which doesn't laugh and very often presents a dead-pan front.

What to choose

1. It should be a character you think you can understand. If the situation is outside the range of your own experience, you should be able to imagine the motivation of your character and draw on those parts of your own nature which can be used to create the rôle.

2. You should choose something about which you are enthusiastic—maybe an experience you can identify with: or it may be the language which gives you a 'lift'. Good writing has a way of raising the actor to its level.

3. Try to find a speech which is complete in itself, which is, as far as possible, self-explanatory. Long introductions are tedious and a waste of precious time.

4. Look for speeches which have a shape, such as a definite climax.

5. Search for the best plays of their kind. There are good and bad black comedies, kitchen comedies, farces, thrillers, period plays, melodramas, burlesques, verse plays and tragedies. The better a speech is written, the easier it will be to make a success of it at an audition. Cheap material has a way of cheapening the performer.

6. Search for the best contemporary writing. There is a wealth of untapped material to be found in plays of today.

7. If you have already chosen a well-born character in Shakespeare, choose also a character who speaks in a moderr idiom and in a more relaxed style. And don't let the old-fashioned bogey of 'Elocution' raise its head during your audition, in any of your work.

8. Finally, be ruthless when deciding what to choose. It is not so much a matter of what you enjoy doing as what you make your audience enjoy: not so much what you feel as what you make your panel of judges feel. Remember they are sitting there hoping to be moved, stirred, excited by what you are creating in front of them.

Preparing the audition speeches

So now we will imagine that you have chosen two contrasted speeches, of the appropriate lengths and ones which you are confident will give you a chance to show what you can do, and what your potential is.

How should you set about preparing them?

1. Allow plenty of time. It is surprising how many people leave learning the lines until the last minute; some even till the night before. You can't even begin to act until you know the lines so well that you don't have to worry about remembering them. Forgetting the lines and having to be continually prompted creates a very bad impression at an audition and is usually fatal to the result.

2. Re-read the *whole* of both plays. Far too many people plunge into audition speeches without studying the full text of the play. The actor has to visualize the situation in the play at the point where the speech occurs and to know what stage of develop-

ment the character has reached at that moment. Obviously this is going to affect the timing, the emotional temperature of the speech and the movement.

3. Don't start learning the lines until you are sure that you fully understand them. It is a good idea, in Shakespeare for example, to turn the whole thing into modern English of the sort you would use yourself, to make sure you understand the words before learning them.

4. Consider the movement and the voice and speech of the character as an integrated whole. The movement must be in character, in period and properly motivated. If possible, try to find out beforehand the size of the acting area that is to be used for the audition.

5. Learn the lines in conjunction with the moves and business. In this way one will help the other and make for an integrated characterisation, involving mind, heart, voice and body.

6. Don't over rehearse. If you do, you will lose freshness and spontaneity and give the kind of artificial, 'drilled' performance which is the very thing that judges dislike most.

Necessary preparation before rehearsal

Steep yourself in the atmosphere of the whole play and try to get inside the skin of your character.

A guide to the rehearsal of speeches

I have broken down two speeches to give you an idea how they

might be approached. Different coaches have different methods and this is only a guide to possible interpretation.

It would be unwise to follow my suggestions exactly, should you choose to perform one of the following two speeches. (In fact I have included the Ayckbourn speech in the list of suggestions for comedy speeches for Drama School auditions.) Other people at the same audition may have read this book and you don't want to give a carbon copy of someone else's performance.

Movement and positioning

I have included rough sketches to show how the two speeches might be positioned and have indicated where the other, imaginary characters might be placed. When you are playing a scene alone on the stage except for an imaginary character it is sensible to put yourself in the dominant position, that is upstage of the other character. I have often seen actors playing an audition scene in dead profile or threequarters back to the audience. This is the one occasion when you can, legitimately 'hog' the stage!

'As You Like It' by William Shakespeare

I HAVE taken a short excerpt from 'As You Like It' to show a possible approach to this scene of romantic comedy. Rosalind, disguised as a boy, has just acted out a mock-marriage ceremony with Orlando. The scene is in prose but has a poetic rhythmical style which may be used to express Rosalind's mercurial changes of mood. As in all the best comedy, it has a touch of underlying heart-break, as when Rosalind reflects on the changing nature of man's and woman's love before and after marriage. The mood is playfully teasing, tender, sad and wildly excited by turns and Rosalind has to suggest these changes swiftly and delicately.

The grassy mound is represented by a chair lying on its side. Orlando is imagined to be moving downstage R after the word 'husband'.

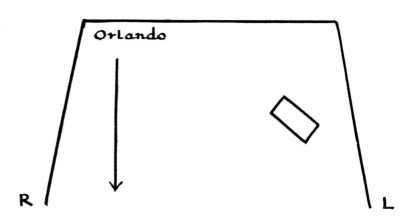

TEXT	INTERPRETATION	MOVES AND BUSINESS
ROSALIND: I might ask you for your commission; but— I do take thee, Orlando, for my husband.[1] There's a girl goes before the priest; and certainly, a woman's thought runs before her actions . . .	She suddenly imagines how this would be 'for real'. Trying to disguise her emotion: apparently light-hearted.	[1]She breaks away stage L
[2]Now tell me how long you would have her, after you have possessed her . . . Say 'a day' without the 'ever'.[3] No, no, Orlando; men are April when they woo, December when they wed: maids are May when they are maids, but the sky changes when they are wives.[4] I will be more jealous of thee than a Barbary cock-pigeon over his hen, more clamorous than a parrot against rain, more new-fangled than an ape, more giddy in my desires than a monkey. I will weep for nothing,[5] like Diana in the fountain, and I will do that when you are dispos'd to be merry; I will laugh like a hyen, and that when thou art inclin'd to sleep . . .	A shade of sadness here Her mood changes to one of wild excitement.	[2]She crosses down R and kneels in front of Orlando. [3]She looks away from Orlando. [4]She moves upstage C [5]She sits on 'mound'.
[6]The wiser the waywarder. Make the doors upon a woman's wit, and it will out at the casement; shut that, and 'twill out at the key-hole; stop that, 'twill fly with the smoke out at the chimney.	Calmer now and enjoying the situation Pace slows down here.	[6]She comes close to Orlando and kneels beside him. She could follow the 'smoke' with her eyes.

16

'Table Manners' by Alan Ayckbourn

This speech, taken from Alan Ayckbourn's trilogy 'The Norman Conquests', is light comedy on the surface, but has an underlying satirical bite. It calls for a light touch, brisk pace but very careful pointing of the lines so that the full impact of what Norman is saying gets over to the audience. The scene is the breakfast table, with the other characters sitting round it in silence, determined to ignore Norman. He is in the dog-house because of his outrageous behaviour of the night before. I have suggested certain inflections on some of the words, but only as a guide to the general sense of the speech:

⟋ implies a rising inflection
⟍ implies a falling inflection

⋁ and ⋀ imply combinations of rising and falling.

This is a more difficult speech to bring off successfully than it would appear to be. It demands sustained vitality and attack but the comedy must not seem to be forced.

As so much of the speech is an unkind attack on Sarah and Annie, and indirectly on Tom, the actor has to be careful not to make the character too unattractive. An audience won't laugh good-humouredly at a character it dislikes. Norman has to have some charm otherwise his success with the women in the play is inexplicable.

However the actor is helped by Ayckbourn's gift for writing speakable dialogue that flows easily.

For the purpose of an audition speech I have imagined the table running up and down centre with Norman's seat at the upstage end of it so that he dominates the imagined characters sitting at either side of it.

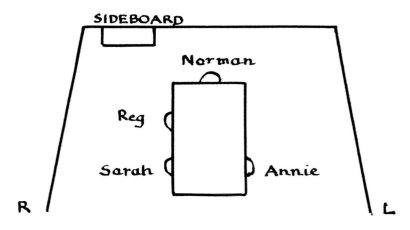

TEXT	INTERPRETATION	MOVES AND BUSINESS

[1]Nothing wrong in a few drinks. Don't speak. I don't care. Going to be a pretty dull Sunday if we all sit in silence, I can tell you. Well, I'm *not* sitting in silence. I'll find something to do. I know, I'll go up and frighten Mother.* Ah-ha! Nearly got you again. Is it too much to ask for something to eat? *It's too much to ask for something to eat†* [2]**May I borrow your bowl? That's awfully nice of you. And your spoon? Thank you. [3] Now then, what shall I have? Puffa Puffa rice Ah-ha . . .[4] No Sunday papers. Dear, dear. Ah well I shall have to read my morning Cereal . . . Do we all get that? Apparently we don't. [5] Stop! Stop everything. Listen. A free pair of pinking shears for only 79p and six Puffa Puffa tokens. Hurry, hurry, hurry. What's this? Is nobody hurrying? Do you mean to tell me that none of you want them? Where's the spirit of British pinking? Dead, presumably. Like my relations.[6] Hang on, I've got another game. Mind reading. I'll read your minds. Now then, where shall we start? Sarah. Sarah is thinking‡—that noisy man up there should be at home with his wife. What is he doing shattering the calm of our peaceful Sunday breakfast with his offers of reduced pinking shears? Why is he here, shouting at us like this?§ *Why isn't he at home, like any other decent husband shouting at his wife?* He came down here to seduce his wife's own sister. How low can he get? ¶the fact that his wife's own sister said, at one stage anyway, that she was perfectly happy to go along with him is beside the point. The fact that *little Annie*

In defiant mood.

*Intended to annoy Annie who is at home looking after her.
He is trying to make them break their silence.
†These two lines should have a rhythm.
**With exaggerated courtesy.

He imitates TV commercials. Mock surprise.

A lift of voice.
A drop
Suggests another bright idea has occurred to him.
Although apparently playful, this 'game' has vicious undertones.
‡He should suggest Sarah's voice here.
§A laugh line, needing a light touch.
¶He presses home his spiteful attack.
¶In his own voice.

[1]He enters and sits at head of the table.

[2]He gets up and moves down R side of table and takes cereal bowl and spoon.
[3]He goes to side-board up R and examines cereal packets.
[4]He sits at top of table and fills his bowl.
[5]He bangs table.

[6]He eats a handful of dry cereal from his bowl.

TEXT	INTERPRETATION	MOVES AND BUSINESS

There should be a rhythm here.
°He turns his attention to Annie.

here was perfectly happy to ditch old reliable Tom—without a second thought—and come off with me is beside the point. We won't mention that because it doesn't quite fit in with the facts as we would like them. °And what is little Annie thinking, I wonder? Maybe furtively admiring my pyjamas, who knows? Pyjamas that could have been hers. With all that they contain. These nearly were mine.

He may be sending himself up slightly here.

Or maybe she is thinking . . .* Phew, that was a close shave. I could have been shacked up in some dreadful hotel with this man—at this very moment . . . what a lucky escape for me. Thank heavens, I am back here at home amidst my talkative family exchanging witty break-fast banter. Knowing my two-legged faithful companion and friend, Tom the rambling vet, is even now planning to propose to me in 1997 just as soon as he's cured our cat. Meanwhile, I can live here peacefully, totally fulfilled, racing up and down stairs looking after Mother, having the time of my life and living happily ever after until I'm fifty-five and fat . . . I'm glad I didn't go to that hotel. **Well, let me tell you so am I. I wouldn't want a weekend with you, any way. And I'll tell you the funniest thing of all, shall I? . . . I didn't even book the hotel. I knew you wouldn't come. You didn't have the guts.

"These nearly were mine" could be sung—mock Al Jolson style perhaps.
*He should suggest Annie's voice here, in contrast to his imitation of Sarah's.

A side-swipe at Tom.
A cruel commentary on Tom and Annie's relationship.

**A complete change here as Norman returns to his natural voice to humiliate Annie.

Annie rushes out

Yelling after her.

By permission of the author and of Chatto & Windus.

Suggestions for audition speeches

In the following list of possible audition material you will find the name of the play and its author and publisher. I have given the act· and scene and the beginnings and endings of the speeches. A few notes of guidance have been added which I hope may be helpful to the actor.

Sometimes you will find that another character has a line or two within the scene but you will find that your character's lines flow naturally if you cut out the other character's. Use your discretion as to what cuts to make to achieve a cohesive unity.

For convenience the list has been divided into sections as follows:

Speeches for women

SUGGESTED MATERIAL FOR AUDITIONS FOR DRAMA SCHOOLS

Straight, serious speeches. See page 21
Comedy speeches. 23
Character speeches. 25
Shakespeare. 28

SUGGESTED MATERIAL FOR DRAMA STUDENTS

Straight, serious speeches. See page 31

Comedy speeches. 33
Character speeches. 35
Shakespeare. 38

Speeches for men

SUGGESTED MATERIAL FOR AUDITIONS FOR DRAMA SCHOOLS

Straight, serious speeches. See page 41
Comedy speeches. 44
Character speeches. 46
Shakespeare. 48

SUGGESTED MATERIAL FOR DRAMA STUDENTS

Straight, serious speeches. See page 50
Comedy speeches. 53
Character speeches. 56
Shakespeare. 58

Speeches for men and women

SUGGESTED MATERIAL FOR AUDITIONS FOR CHILDREN'S THEATRE

See page 60

Speeches for Women: *Suggested Material for Drama Schools*

STRAIGHT, SERIOUS SPEECHES

ABSENT FRIENDS Alan Ayckbourn *Chatto & Windus* *French, New York*	Diana	Act II	From "When I was a little girl . . ." To "I want to join the Mounted Police."	She is emotional and highly strung. The speech needs careful shaping to its climax at the end.
CITY SUGAR Stephen Poliakov *French*	Nicola	Scene 7	From "The last . . . the last pop concert I went to." To ". . . but it was great."	A fan of a pop group describes one of their concerts. The acting has to be sensitive in order to bring out the pathos in the character.
THE DEVILS John Whiting *French*	Sister Jeanne	Act I	From "My dear Sister: it is with great regret . . ." To "Is that it? . . . Is that it?"	Jeanne, a hump-backed nun, sees in her imagination Grandier making love and experiences the love-making vicariously. A highly charged emotional speech which calls for technical control.
EASTER August Strindberg *Cape*	Eleonora	Act I	From "Shall I tell you something more about the birds?" To "I took the flower, and went out."	This disturbed child of the universe describes the language of the birds and flowers in a poetic speech. A very young appearance and the ability to create a child-like vision are needed.
THE GOOD PERSON OF SZECHWAN Bertolt Brecht *Eyre Methuen* *French, New York*	Shen Teh	Scene 7	From "Oh joy! A small being is coming to life in my body." To ". . . got his own bite in first."	Translations of this vary in quality; it is worth comparing them. Shen Teh talks to her unborn son. The speech has opportunities for mime and singing and has a grave beauty.

FEAR & MISERY IN THE 3RD REICH Bertolt Brecht *Grove Press Inc* *New York*	The Jewish Wife		From "Yes, I'm going now Fritz." To "I love you really."	As she packs before leaving Germany, the Jewish Wife rehearses the speech she is going to make to her husband. The imaginary husband has to be conjured up. Careful control of pace and pitch and realistic mime are required.
KENNEDY'S CHILDREN R. Patrick *French*	Wanda	Act I	From "To me it was the most important day of my life." To ". . . God rest his soul."	Wanda remembers the day in the office on which President Kennedy was assassinated. A speech of emotional recall. The American accent shouldn't be overdone. The style is vividly colloquial.
THE PARTY Jane Arden *French*	Henrietta	Act II Scene 2	From "Father? Which would you like?" To ". . . a beautiful cry that really shows he's somebody."	A speech which can be highly effective and deeply moving, or, on the other hand deeply embarrassing. Sentimentality must be avoided and any hint of 'winsomeness'. Henrietta is acting out the party she would like to be giving for her father on his return from treatment for alcoholism.
THE QUEEN AND THE REBELS Ugo Betti (trans. Henry Reed) *French*	Argia	Act IV	From "What you're saying in fact . . ." To "I am as I would always have wished to be."	Argia is a slut who has been mistaken for the Queen. The speech gives an opportunity to show a strong contrast between the bitter, earthy first part and the lyrical, yearning mood at the end.
TRANSLATIONS Brian Friel *Faber and Faber* *French, New York*	Maire		From "Honest to God I must be going off my head.," To "It didn't last long did it?"	This young Southern Irish girl is in love with an Englishman. A tender and moving speech.

Speeches for Women: *Suggested Material for Drama Schools*

COMEDY

ABSENT FRIENDS Alan Ayckbourn *French*	Diana	Act I	From "Well I'm glad you could come this afternoon." To ". . . when they're playing at home."	Diana, slightly strained, is speaking obliquely to the woman her husband is having an affair with. Ayckbourn is also satirising cliché-ridden contemporary conversation.
GILT AND GINGERBREAD Lionel Hale *Evans*	Louise	Act I	From "I call it a damned outrage." To "Well, don't go!"	The style of the speech is light, sophisticated comedy. Although pretending to be angry with the young man who has followed her, Louise is secretly flattered. There is a steady build to the climax at the end—which is followed by an anti-climax.
A JUBILEE Anton Chekov *Penguin*	Tatiana		From "Darling! Did you miss me?" To "The weather was wonderful."	This speech calls for bubbling vitality but also a light touch. It has to be played very fast. The lines have to be carefully pointed to avoid a gabbling effect.
LITTLE MALCOLM AND HIS STRUGGLE AGAINST THE EUNUCHS David Halliwell *French*	Ann	Scene 11	From "'ow would you like to shaft me?" To "But there's no future in being subtle with you."	This North Country girl is having great fun in teasing the self-styled campus 'stud' and exploding the myth of his virility. It is essential that the scene be played with good humour and not maliciously. The speech is cut up a good deal but will flow if the other character's lines are omitted.

NEXT TIME I'LL SING TO YOU James Saunders *Andre Deutsch*	Lizzie		From "Come let us sport us while we may . . ." To "Only I just don't want to."	Lizzie is an amusing little cockney sparrow. Here she is laying down her views on love and marriage.
ONCE A CATHOLIC Mary O'Malley *Amber Lane Press*	Mother Peter	Scene 13 & 14	From "Why would anyone go into the toilet to read the bible?" To ". . . will be banned from taking their O levels."	Mother Peter is a middle-aged Southern Irish teaching nun. The speech has to be spoken with earnest solemnity.
THE PASSING OUT PARADE Anne Valery *French*	Sergeant Pickering	Act I Scene 7	From "Right, me anguished amateurs" To "Jenkins, Left, right. Left, right. LEFT, right."	The sergeant is demonstrating a salute to A.T.S. recruits in early 1944. She is very keen and peppers her speech with French phrases in a spirit of mock gaiety.
THE PRIME OF MISS JEAN BRODIE Jay Presson Allen *(adapted from Muriel Spark)* *French*	Miss Brodie	Act II	From "There is very little for me to say . . ." To "Good day, Miss Mackay."	This should be played in a refined Edinburgh accent. Miss Brodie has little humour and here is angrily outraged.
THE RULING CLASS Peter Barnes *Heinemann* *French, New York*	Grace	Scene 14	From "I always get first night nerves" To "riding a one-wheel bike on his wedding night."	During this speech Grace starts to strip in a provocative but utterly unselfconscious way. The requisites for this scene are confidence, a good body and charm.
THE STAR-SPANGLED GIRL Neil Simon *Avon* *Random House*	Sophie	Act I Scene 2	From "Excuse me, Mr Cornell, Ah have tried to be neighborly!" To ". . . leave me ay-lone!"	Sophie is described as "a lovely young blonde prototype of the all-American girl." She exudes freshness and vitality and superb health.

Speeches for Women: *Suggested Material for Drama Schools*

CHARACTER

BOESMAN AND LENA Athol Fugard *Oxford University Press* *French, New York*	Lena	Act II	From "You shouldn't have hit him, Boesman." To "But not so fast. It's dark."	She is black, is in her fifties and has an Africaans accent. A strong, bitterly accusing speech in which she gives Boesman her view of their relationship.
CALL ME A LIAR John Mortimer *Methuen*	Girl		From "I wanted to make them be happy those children." To "Do you think I started it?" **THEN** From "In Notting Hill Gate . . ." To "Now I feel happy."	A German au ·pair girl is describing the two different kinds of treatment she has been getting in two different English homes. Opportunity is given to convey two strongly contrasted moods.
MARBLE ARCH (from **COME AS YOU ARE**) John Mortimer *French*	Laura		From "Max! Max! What's happened to you in there, Max?" To "Have you dropped dead in there? Oh—Max,—you have!"	Laura is "one-time toast of the Rank Organisation, Queen of Pinewood and star of a dozen forgotten British movies." She is in her bedroom talking to her lover, Max, who is in the bathroom and has had a heart attack. Making up and dressing business has to be carefully timed with the comedy lines.
MISALLIANCE George Bernard Shaw *Penguin* *French, New York*	Lina		From "Old pal: this is a stuffy house." To ". . . he shall not buy Lina Szczepanowska."	A Czech lion tamer gives vent to her views on Englishmen and marriage. A rhetorical speech which needs careful shaping to its major and minor climaxes. The broken accent has to be sustained. Her movement is vigorous.

THE NIGHT OF THE IGUANA Tennessee Williams *Crown Publishers Inc* *New York*	Hannah	Act III	From "Yes, I have had two experiences—well, encounters." To "... A love experience? Yes I do call it one."	Hannah is described as "thirty to forty ... almost timeless—androgynous looking". This is a long scene which could be conveniently cut into two sections. It requires intense concentration. The character should emerge as brave and pathetic, deserving of sympathy.
A NIGHT OUT Harold Pinter *Methuen*	The Girl	Act III Scene 2	From "Come in. Don't slam the door." To "I haven't ... spoken to anyone for some hours."	She is a complex character, desperately lonely in London. Although she is a tart, she tries to bolster herself up with illusions of gentility. This facade often cracks during the scene. She must be seen to react to the other character's lines.
PORTRAIT OF A QUEEN William Francis *French*	Victoria		From "The crown being placed on my head ..." To "at length—with great pain."	This is Queen Victoria's own account of her coronation. This speech should not be obviously played for laughs; the comedy arises from her repeated references to Lord Melbourne. These need only to be heightened slightly. Victorian precision of speech and youthful dignity are called for.
THE RAINMAKER N. Richard *Nash* *French*	Lizzie	Act I	From "Pop, let's not beat about the bush." To "Can I help it if I was good in geography?"	Lizzie is a strong, forthright girl with a wry sense of humour. Some charm should emerge, however. She should not be played aggressively.

26

STEVIE Hugh Whitemore *French*	Stevie	Act II	From "The most exciting thing of all . . ." To "And the young naval man gets a taxi for you."	The late Stevie Smith describes her visit to the Palace to receive the Queen's Gold Medal for Poetry. Although the speech is written in slightly satirical style the satire should not be made ill-natured. If it is, the comedy will be lost. Stevie's quirky eccentricity should be suggested without caricature.
WHO'S AFRAID OF VIRGINIA WOOLF? Edward Albee *Penguin* *Athenavar*	Martha	Act III	From "hey, hey . . . Where is everybody . . .?" To "Martha, you'll be a song-writer yet."	Martha is a large boisterous woman of fifty two, looking somewhat younger. She is an alcoholic. The speech calls for a virtuoso performance, with its sudden swings of mood. The inebriation should not be overdone; sometimes she sobers down and shows us "the dark night of her soul."

Speeches for Women: *Suggested Material for Drama Schools*

SHAKESPEARE

AS YOU LIKE IT Act IV Scene 1	Rosalind	From "Alas, dear love, I cannot lack thee two hours!" To "I'll go find a shadow, and sigh till he come."	A scene of romantic comedy. Rosalind, as Ganymede, teases Orlando and after he goes is swept off her feet with love of him.
THE COMEDY OF ERRORS Act II Scene 2	Adriana	From "Ay, ay, Antipholus, look strange and frown." To "I live dis-stain'd, thou undishonoured."	A lively comedy speech in which Adriana reproaches the man she believes to be her husband. The thought process in her argument has to be clearly brought out.
CYMBELINE Act III Scene 6	Imogen	From "I see a man's life is a tedious one." To "Such a foe, good heavens!"	This charming heroine is en route to meet her husband. She is disguised as a boy. The speech combines pathos with comedy.
HENRY IV PART II Act II Scene 1	Hostess	From "Marry, if thou wert an honest man . . ." To "Deny it, if thou canst."	Mistress Quickly is railing at Falstaff in a scene which requires sustained pace and vitality. Her Cockney accent should not be overdone.
HENRY IV PART II Act II Scene 3	Lady Percy	From "O, yet, for God's sake, go not to these wars!" To "Have talk'd of Monmouth's grave."	Lady Percy rebukes her father-in-law for wanting to support his allies, when he withheld support from his own son. She remembers her dead husband with love and pride.

28

RICHARD III Act IV Scene 1	Anne	From "And I with all unwillingness will go." To "And will, no doubt, shortly be rid of me."	Anne, the unhappy wife of Richard III is on her way to see the two young Princes at the tower, when she is summoned to Westminster to be crowned Queen. She remembers how she once cursed Richard's wife and realises now that that curse has fallen on her.
ROMEO AND JULIET Act III Scene 2	Juliet	From "What devil art thou that dost torment me thus?" To "O, that deceit should dwell In such a gorgeous palace!"	A highly emotional scene in which Juliet is swept by conflicting passions. First she believes that Romeo has been killed and then learns that it is Tybalt who has been slain—and by Romeo's hand. The Nurse's lines have to be suggested by Juliet's reactions.
THE TWO GENTLE- MEN OF VERONA Act IV Scene 3	Silvia	From "O Eglamour, thou art a gentleman—" To "That I may venture to depart alone."	Silvia, the Duke's daughter is in love with Valentine. He has been banished and in this speech Silvia entreats Sir Eglamour to help her escape to join her love. A confidential conspiratorial style is needed. She has to exert persuasive charm on Sir Eglamour.
THE WINTER'S TALE Act III Scene 2	Hermione	From "Sir, spare your threats." To "Apollo be my judge!"	Hermione, Queen of Sicilia, has been falsely accused of adultery by her husband Leontes. Here she is facing him in open Court. In spite of her humiliation by him, she has great dignity and spiritual strength although she is physically weak, having just given birth to her daughter.

Act IV
Scene 4

Perdita

From "Sir, welcome."
To "And welcome to our shearing."
THEN
From "Here's flow'rs for you:"
To "To strew him o'er and o'er!"

Perdita, having escaped the death plotted for her by Leontes, has been brought up by a shepherd as his daughter. Here she is acting as hostess at a country festival. She is talking to two middle aged men, Polixenes and Camillo and to young Florizel whom she loves. This speech contains some of Shakespeare's finest lyrical writing and the verse-form should be preserved without sacrifice of naturalness and spontaneous freshness.

Speeches for Women: *Suggested Material for Drama Students*

STRAIGHT, SERIOUS SPEECHES

CAMINO REAL Tennessee Williams *Penguin*	Marguerite	Block 10 .	From "Oh, Jacques, we're used to each other." To "But tenderness, the violets in the mountains—can't break the rocks!"	Marguerite Gautier (La Dame Aux Camélias) is talking to Casanova in the limbo where they both find themselves after death. An emotional, wistful speech that calls for a sense of period.
THE CAUCASIAN CHALK CIRCLE Bertolt Brecht *Methuen* *Random House and* *French, New York*	Grusha	Scene 6	From "Even if you were thirty . . ." To ". . . swinging from the gallows."	A passionate and violent speech, deliberately coarse and crude: it needs playing in an ugly way.
DANTON'S DEATH Georg Büchner *Oxford Paperbacks*	Marion	Scene 4	From "No, let me be . . ." To "The people that get the most pleasure have to pay the most."	She is talking to Danton about her initiation into sex. They are on a bed in her room at the Palais Royal.
DUET FOR ONE Tom Kempinski *French*	Stephanie	Act I	From "Hey diddle diddle" To "Vat do you sink and feel hum?"	Stephanie, who is suffering from multiple sclerosis is bitterly attacking her psychiatrist: The underlying hurt which causes the aggression should be shown.
FLINT David Mercer *Methuen*	Dixie	Act II Scene 4	From "No, sir, I have no means of support." To "Pom tiddley om pom Pom."	Dixie, who has just had a baby, talks about Flint, killed in a motor-cycle crash. This is an understated speech demanding an intensity which shows underlying depth of feeling.

JUMPERS Tom Stoppard *Faber & Faber* *French, New York*	Dorothy	Act I	From "Poor moon man falling home like Lucifer . . ." To "I should never have mentioned unicorns to a Freudian." THEN From "Unfortunately I don't feel so good today." To "Oh, yes, things were in place then."	An extrovert young woman, an ex-dancer, expresses her sense of disillusion in an unromantic world of changing values. Some mood changes here and a powerful emotional climax.
MISS JULIE August Strindberg (trans. Michael Meyer) *Secker & Warburg* *French, New York*	Julie		From "Now try to be calm; Christine . . ." To ". . . or somewhere else."	After she has lost her virginity to her father's valet, Jean, the disillusioned Julie tries half hysterically to plan a future for herself, Jean and Christine. Sustained attack and febrile nervous intensity are the keys to this.
THE OLD ONES Arnold Wesker *Jonathan Cape* *French, New York*	Rosa	Act II Scene 8	From "I'm here once and once only . . ." To "*There-is-no-other.*"	Rosa is a Ministry of Education careers advisory officer. Here, in exasperation she lets fly at a group of apathetic boys. There is a change of mood at the end when she tries to persuade them of the value of books.
ONDINE Jean Giraudoux *French*	Ondine	Act III	From "You used to laugh at me . . ." To "I shall be true to you always."	Ondine, the water-sprite is bidding her human lover goodbye before returning to the waters. Lyrical grace of movement is demanded.
UNCLE VANYA Anton Chekov *Penguin* *French, New York*	Yeliena	Act III	From "There's nothing worse than knowing someone's secret . . ." To ". . . to ask her forgiveness and cry . . ."	The bored wife of a retired professor muses on her own feelings for Astrov and his for her. This is quietly reflective and calls for a sense of period style in speech and movement.

32

Speeches for Women: *Suggested Material for Drama Students*

COMEDY

CAT ON A HOT TIN ROOF Tennessee Williams *Secker & Warburg*	Maggie	Act I	From "Did anyone ever tell you that you're an ass-aching Puritan Brick?" To "Somebody spit tobacco juice in her face."	Maggie speaks fast, but at the same time in a drawling way. Her anecdote is aimed at Brick although she realises that he is not reacting to it—nor to her. The speech is drily humorous and sad at the same time.
EDUCATING RITA Willy Russell *French*	Rita	Act II Scene 1	From "Frank, it was fantastic . . ." To "I'm dead familiar with Chekhov now."	Rita is a disarmingly frank and natural North Country girl who has an exuberant vitality.
IF YOU'RE GLAD I'LL BE FRANK Tom Stoppard *Faber & Faber* *French, New York*	Gladys	Scene 2	From "I can hear, them all . . ." To "Oh Frank! Help me!"	The Post Office's Talking Clock alternates her official duties with a cri de coeur to her boy friend. This must, of course, be played with real feeling and earnestness; the comedy comes from Stoppard's inventive, witty dialogue.
OFFICE SUITE Alan Bennett *Faber & Faber*	Doreen		From "You never know anybody, do you?" To "Don't work too hard."	A North Country office girl chatting on the phone. The more natural and convincing she is the better will the comedy come over.
ONCE A CATHOLIC Mary O'Malley *Amber Press*	Mother Peter	Act I	From "Now you all know what this is." To "This irreligious girl."	Mother Peter is sternly lecturing the girls on the importance of wearing the Mother Fatima 'knicker'. She is completely serious. A Southern Irish accent is essential for this speech.

33

PLAZA SUITE Neil Simon *French*	Norma	Act III	From "Hello? Hello operator. Can I have the Blue Room, please." To "And Heaven help the three of us."	The anguished Bride's mother tries to persuade her husband to come up to help her get their daughter out of the bathroom. She has locked herself in. Pace, good timing, above all a sense of desperation are all demanded by this speech. The American accent should not be exaggerated.
PRESENT LAUGHTER Noel Coward *French*	Joanna	Act II Scene 1	From "Shut up! You must be fair." To "... the most passionately attractive man I have ever known in all my life."	A short but effective speech. The alluring Joanna tries to seduce her former flame. A slowish pace and a build-up of intensity are needed. There should be a sensuous use of voice and body.
THE SEA Edward Bond *Eyre-Methuen*	Mary	Scene 4	From "Jessica hand out the books." To "No, no. I cannot bear it." (Omit the other characters' lines)	The dominant Mrs Rafi is taking a rehearsal of 'Orpheus and Euridice' with an almost exclusively female cast. She is an ebullient and larger then life-size character. But care should be taken not to go over the top.
THE SLEEPING PRINCE Terence Rattigan *French*	Mary	Act I Scene 1	From "Say listen—I could do with a small one, too." To "Do they all fall as easily as that, the Maisies and the others!"	Mary, an American shop-girl is being entertained by the Arch-Duke who has just made an unsuccessful pass at her. Naturally no attempt should be made to imitate Marilyn Monroe in the part, but a bubbling sense of fun is needed.
TIGER AT THE GATES Jean Giraudoux (trans. Christopher Fry) *Methuen*	Helen		From "You are being very difficult . . ." To ". . . there is always you and Hector Andromache."	The legendary Helen of Troy is talking to Andromache in a wickedly provocative way. Here she is shown as a wit as well as a beauty. The movement needs to be poised and flowing.

34

Speeches for Women: *Suggested Material for Drama Students*

CHARACTER

ALL GOD'S CHILLUN GOT WINGS Eugene O'Neill *Jonathan Cape*	Ella	Act II Scene 3	From "I'll give you the laugh, wait and see!" To "Why don't you let Jim and I be happy?"	A poor white girl living in New York is married to a black man. She is subject to murderous fits of mania, punctuated by more lucid moments. This has to be played from deep inner feeling. The disturbed condition of Ella may be shown by disorientated movement and facial expression.
BLOOD WEDDING Federico Lorca *Penguin*	The Mother	Act III Scene 2	From "Hush, I said." To "Blessed be God, who stretches us out to rest."	A passionately lyrical speech. The Mother, mourning her dead son, turns on her daughter-in-law. Her lines are considerably cut up by other characters' dialogue, but can be joined to flow.
FILUMENA Eduardo de Filippo *French*	Filumena	Act III	From "Listen to me, Dummi', . . ." To "We can still go our separate ways."	The volatile Filumena, now middle-aged, explains to the father of one of her three sons why she can't tell him which one is his. The 'tune' of broken Italian has to be caught. There should be an expressive use of hands.
MOLLY Simon Gray *French*	Molly	Act II Scene 3	From "Oh, who are you?" To ". . . Spurting . . . spurting, do you see?"	Eve is heavily sedated in this scene. She also has a drinking problem. The play is based on the Rattenbury murder case. In this scene she finds her housekeeper being interviewed by the police.

NIGHT AND DAY Tom Stoppard *French*	Ruth	Act I	From "I despise them. Not foreign correspondents of course." To "The rhinoceros or the rhinoceros bird?"	An attractive, intelligent and sophisticated character. Ruth is in her late thirties.
THE SEA Edward Bond *Eyre-Methuen*	Mrs Rafi	Scene 7	From "I'm afraid of getting old." To "No I've thrown my life away."	The ageing Mrs Rafi, at present a dynamic, forceful character, has a vision of herself in old age—helpless and dependent on other people. Too much self-pity should be avoided.
THE SHADOW OF THE GLEN J. M. Synge. *French*	Nora		From "It's in a lonesome place . . ." To ". . . but it's a queer thing surely."	Rich Irish comedy set in Wicklow. Nora's husband, supposedly dead is lying on a bed in the corner covered with a sheet. It is important to capture the lilting rhythms and fine balance of the lines.
SOMETHING UNSPOKEN Tennessee Williams *Curtis Brown*	Cornelia		From "Are you upstairs now, dear?" To ". . . as soon as there's something to tell me."	Cornelia lives in the Garden District of New Orleans. She is a formidable matriarch of the Daughters of America school. This telephone conversation needs to be played with feverish anxiety in case she is not elected unopposed as Regent. The style is satirical comedy.
UNDER MILK WOOD Dylan Thomas *Dent* *French, New York*	Mrs Dai Bread One and Mrs Dai Bread Two		From "Me, Mrs Dai Bread One, capped and shawled and no old corset," To ". . . scowling at the sunshine, lighting up my pipe."	A good audition speech if the Welsh accent is convincing. It combines two short speeches and gives an opportunity to show contrasted characterisation. The first character is cosy and relaxed and the second unconventional, seductive, with a hint of gypsy beauty.

36

THE WHITE LIARS
Peter Shaffer
Hamish Hamilton
French, New York

Sophie

From "Mister, I know I don't look so prosperous . . ."
To "I'll read his fortune, mister! I'll read it for him!"

Sophie was once beautiful and is still handsome. She has a strong but always understandable German accent. This calls for strong characterisation.

Speeches for Women: *Suggested Material for Drama Students*

SHAKESPEARE

ANTONY AND CLEOPATRA ACT V SCENE 2	Cleopatra	From "Sir, I will eat no meat;" To "As this I dreamt of?" THEN From "No matter, sir, what I have heard or known." To "Think you there was or might be such a man As this I dreamed of!"	Cleopatra has been taken captive. The first part of the scene gives opportunities to show fiery defiance and the second part, spoken to Dolabella, is spoken in a mood of almost languorous, wistful, loving pride. A big-scale performance is called for.
CORIOLANUS ACT V SCENE 3	Volumnia	From "Speak to me, son." To "And then I'll speak a little."	Volumnia, mother of Coriolanus, speaks to her son, begging him to spare Rome. She has great authority. The speech makes demands on vocal resources.
CYMBELINE Act IV Scene 2	Imogen	From "Yes, sir, to Milford Haven. Which is the way?" To ". . . O, my lord, my lord!"	A highly dramatic scene in which Imogen half drugged, awakes to find the body of a headless man beside her, whom she takes to be her husband. It is important to play it simply and with restraint. A difficult but challenging speech.
HENRY IV PART II SCENE 4	Doll Tearsheet	From "Charge me! I scorn you, scurvy companion." To "Therefore captains had need look to't."	Doll Tearsheet is Falstaff's drinking companion and doxy. Here she is haranguing Pistol with a fine flow of invective which should be relished by the performer. The movement should be loose and provocative.

HENRY V Act II Scene 3	Hostess	From "Nay, sure, he's not in hell:" To ". . . as cold as any stone."	Mistress Quickly's moving account of Falstaff's death. It is clinically accurate in detail and should not be hurried. Any temptation to get a cheap laugh out of ". . . and so upward and upward, and all was as cold as any stone" should be resisted.
KING HENRY VI **PART III** Act V Scene 4	Margaret	From "Great lords, wise men ne'er sit and wail their loss," To "'Twere childish weakness to lament or fear."	The formidable and now ageing Queen Margaret is trying to inject some spirit into her son, Somerset and Oxford. A speech calling for tremendous gusto. It needs to be shaped to its various climaxes. The vivid imagery has to be seen in the mind's eye.
KING JOHN Act III Scene 4	Constance	From "Thou art not holy to belie me so." To "The different plague of each calamity." THEN From "And, father Cardinal, I have heard you say" To "My widow-comfort, and my sorrow's cure!"	Constance, the mother of Prince Arthur who is in the Tower, tries to persuade King Philip and Cardinal Pandulph that she is not mad, even while she is tearing her hair. A lyrically written scene which demands the release of feeling, and the ability to convey madness by disorientated movement.
KING LEAR Act IV Scene 7	Cordelia	From "O my dear father!" To "He wakes; speak to him."	A short but difficult speech. Cordelia's gentleness and strength of character have both to be conveyed. The description of her voice must be borne in mind 'ever soft, gentle and low'. A great compassion colours all her words here.

| TITUS ANDRONICUS Act II Scene 3 | Tamora | From "Have I not reason, think you, to look pale?" To "Or be ye not hence forth call'd my children." | Tamora, Queen of the Goths, tells her children how she has been threatened with death. At the end she calls on them to revenge her. This is a colourfully written speech that needs playing with passion, but control. |
| THE WINTER'S TALE Act III Scene 3 | Paulina | From "Woe the while!" To ". . . and vengeance for't Not dropp'd down yet." | Paulina confronts Leontes with a list of his misdeeds. The speech steadily builds to its climax at the end. |

Speeches for Men: *Suggested Material for Drama Schools*

STRAIGHT, SERIOUS SPEECHES

ANOTHER COUNTRY Julian Mitchell *Amber Lane Press*	Bennett	Act I Scene 4	From "Hell! God I thought you were Fowley . . ." To "It's so wonderful being in love."	Bennett is seventeen and in a state of euphoria. The 1930's public schoolboy image should not be overdrawn, but a good and natural-sounding type of voice and speech is essential.
CHILDREN OF A LESSER GOD Mark Medoff *Dramatists Play Service Inc*	James	Act II	From "You think I'm going to let you change my children into people like you . . ." To "Join. Unjoined."	James is a speech teacher at a State School for the deaf. The play takes place in his mind. The latter half of this speech is in signs. He is talking to Sarah who is deaf and does not lip-read.
THE COMEDIANS Trevor Griffiths *Faber & Faber* *French, New York*	Gethin Price	Act II	From "I wish I had a train . . ." To "Still—made the buggers laugh."	Gethin is about twenty eight and has been to a school for comedians. He is dressed half as Grock, the clown and half as a bovver boy. The speech is sad and bitter and is played in front of a club audience.
DANTON'S DEATH Georg Buchner *Oxford Paperbacks*	Danton	Act IV Scene 3	From "Will the clock not be still?" To ". . .there must be a great grief in the eye that shed them."	Danton is in the prison of the Conciergerie. He is to be guillotined the next day. He is contemplating his death and the nature of dying as the clock ticks inexorably on. Self-pity is to be avoided at all costs.

DUTCHMAN Leroi Jones *Faber & Faber* *French, New York*	Clay		From "I'm not telling you again." To "It's you that's doing the kissing."	Clay is black, aged twenty. Here he is giving vent to his anger and frustration about racial discrimination. He is talking to a white girl. The emotion is violent but has to be controlled by the actor.
KENNEDY'S **CHILDREN** Robert Patrick *French*	Mark	Act I	From "Dear Buddha . . ." To ". . . so that one man can finally be saved."	Mark is on drugs and is remembering an experience he had during the war in Vietnam. It is a short but intensely emotional speech, punctuated by pauses during which he re-lives the scene he is describing.
LUTHER John Osborne *Evans*	Martin	Act II Scene 6	From "I have been served with a piece of paper." To ". . . my mighty fortress, breathe into me."	The first part of this speech is delivered from a pulpit. It is a tirade of powerful invective against the Papal Bull which has just been served on Luther. A strong, flexible voice is required. The second part is a desperate appeal to God to help him.
THE REAR COLUMN Simon Gray *Eyre-Methuen* *French, New York*	Jameson	Act III	From "It's a cannibal feast . . ." To ". . . evidently blinded me to the—the—I'm sorry."	The play is based on a historical incident in the Congo in the 1880's. Jameson, an army officer is describing his reactions to cannibalism.

| THE SEAGULL
Anton Chekhov
Oxford University Press
Hartsdale House
New York | Constantine
Treplev | Act I | From "She loves me, she loves me not."
To "They only put up with me because I'm her son." | Constantine is expressing his pain at his mother's indifference to him. Then he starts thinking of the rut that the theatre is in in Russia. Something of Chekhov's own passionate feelings on the subject emerge. Sustained mental vitality is required. |
| THE WHITE LIARS
Peter Shaffer
French | Tom | | From "How does it work? Colours, isn't it?"
To "I went to bed with her to get dry. Honest." | Tom, a young man is telling a fortune-teller how he was turned into a pop idol. He sometimes reverts into a strong Yorkshire accent. His mood grows into desperation as he proceeds. |

Speeches for Men: *Suggested Material for Drama Schools*

COMEDY

ABSURD PERSON SINGULAR Alan Ayckbourn *French*	Ronald	Act III	From "You seem to have got things prettily organised on the home front . . ." To ". . . want another of those."	Light comedy. Apparently conversational style needed but careful pointing of the lines and a brisk pace.
AH, WILDERNESS! Eugene O'Neill *French*	Richard	Act IV Scene 2	From "Must be nearly nine . . ." To "Gosh, time passes—when you're thinking."	The play is set in Connecticut in 1906. Richard is waiting for his first 'date' to meet him. The mood is a mixture of anxious anticipation and the romantic longing of a sixteen year old.
THE DOCTOR George Melly (Mixed Doubles) *Methuen*	The Doctor		From "Well, try to cut down on your smoking, Mr Taylor." To "Come back for more when you've swallowed these."	A comically satirical monologue in which a doctor hurries through his appointments with three patients. The business has to be carefully timed.
THE HEADMASTER George Melly (Mixed Doubles) *Methuen*	The Headmaster		From "Ye Gods and little fishes!" To "I shall now beat the entire school starting with the Captain of the first fifteen."	He is very angry and paces up and down during this. He must appear to be in dead earnest.
LITTLE MALCOLM AND HIS STRUGGLE AGAINST THE EUNUCHS David Halliwell *French*	Scrawdyke	Act I	From "Look the issue's simple." To "Are we goin' t'go on talkin' for ever!"	Scrawdyke is twenty five and bearded. He likes to think of himself as powerfully sexual. He has a north country accent.

THE NORMAN CONQUESTS (TABLE MANNERS) Alan Ayckbourn *French*	Norman	Act I Scene 2	From "What have we got for breakfast then?" To "You didn't have the guts."	A lively speech. Norman is full of vitality and here he is in a cruelly teasing mood. A fast pace and sustained attack are needed and a sense of rhythm and timing.
PRIVATES ON PARADE Peter Nichols *Faber & Faber French, New York*	Major Flack	Act II Scene 4	From "Right, well done, fall out, gather round."	Flack, a hearty major is briefing his men about jungle warfare. A broad, but not laboured style is required for this speech.
PROFESSIONAL FOUL Tom Stoppard *Faber & Faber*	Stone	Scene 5	From "The confusion which often arises from the ambiguity of ordinary language . . ." To "And here I think the idea of a logical language which can only be unambiguous breaks down."	The character is an American philosopher. The speech is an amusing play with words. Stoppard is evidently enjoying an exploration of one of his favourite themes.
THE REAL INSPECTOR HOUND Tom Stoppard *Faber & Faber French, New York*	Moon		From "It will follow me to the grave . . ." To ". . .stand-ins of the world stand up!"	A short but showy speech. Moon, the second string dramatic critic is in a rebellious mood.
THE TEAHOUSE OF THE AUGUST MOON John Patrick *Heinemann*	Sakini	Act 1 Scene 1	From "Tooti-fruitie." To ". . . splendid example of benevolent assimilation of democracy by Okinawa."	Sakini is Japanese, an interpreter. Here he is contrasting Okinawan civilisation with American. A subtle use of inflection is called for and a broken accent.

Speeches for Men: *Suggested Material for Drama Schools*

AMADEUS Peter Shaffer *Andre Deutsch* *French, New York*	Salieri	Act I Scene 5	From "And then, right away, the concert began." To ". . . and it was the voice of an obscene child."	Salieri, Court Musician, becomes aware of the genius of Mozart. He is appalled that God should have given this gift to 'an obscene child'. He is profoundly disturbed. The speech demands a sense of period in voice and movement.
BECKET Jean Anouilh *Methuen* *French, New York*	King Henry II	Act I	From "If you think I'm in the mood for praying at the moment . . ." To "That's another thing you were better at than me . . ."	Henry is praying at the tomb of Thomas à Becket and remembering the roistering days of their youth. He is telling Thomas about the problems of kingship. The words call for dynamic energy and 'bite' in the earlier part and nostalgic feeling in the latter.
THE DEATH OF BESSIE SMITH Edward Albee *French*	Jack	Scene 2	From "Hey, Bessie, c'mon now . . ." To "We're goin' North again."	Jack is a forty five year old black man. A deep voice is helpful and a strong sense of rhythm. He is strongly persuasive.
THE DRESSER Ronald Harwood *Amber Lane* *French, New York*	Norman	Act I	From "I want to sit with him and be with him." To "The next day he asked if I'd be his dresser."	Norman is devoted to 'Sir' (This part was modelled on Sir Donald Wolfit). He is by turns exasperated and exhilarated by his job as dresser and has a profound affection for him. Neither the effeminacy in the character nor the North Country accent should be exaggerated.

FORGET ME NOT LANE Peter Nichols *Faber & Faber* *French, New York*	Frank	Act II	From "His death made me feel the likelihood . . ." To ". . . and it was so unfair!"	Frank is between thirty and forty. He is bored and disillusioned with his marriage and aware of the increasing unfulfillment of the years ahead.
GETTING ON Alan Bennett *French*	George	Act I	From "How does it happen?" To "And make me a decent man, O God. Amen."	George is middle-aged and is contemplating the ageing process in a speech of witty acerbity. The actor must be able to speak it incisively. The mood changes into genuine emotion.
IF THERE WEREN'T ANY BLACKS YOU'D HAVE TO INVENT THEM Johnny Speight *Methuen*	The Vicar	Part II	From "That's got nothing to do with the colour bar." To "Keep Heaven pure white."	The more believable and sincere the Vicar appears, the more effectively will the satire in this speech come over.
NIGHT MUST FALL Emlyn Williams *Heinemann* *French, New York*	Dan	Act III	From "My life? . . . Well . . . the day don't start so good . . ." To "I don't know what to do. I don't know."	Dan is a young man employed as a page-boy. This is a showy, dramatically effective speech which ranges from near hysteria to crafty coolness. He has a rough accent, indeterminate but more Welsh than anything else.
RHINOCEROS Eugene Ionesco *French*	Berenger	Act III	From "Men aren't so bad-looking, you know." To "I'm not capitulating."	A difficult but splendidly rewarding speech for the actor. It demands considerable vocal and physical resources. It ends with a moving affirmation of the ordinary man's determination to remain an individual and not be swept away with the herd.
SHRIVINGS Peter Shaffer *Penguin*	Mark	Act I Scene 1	From "Have you seen the Ruffian at work?" To "I could. But I wanted another drink."	Mark is a celebrated poet, violent and self-lacerating. He is describing a riot in what appears, at the end, to be an ambivalent mood.

Speeches for Men: *Suggested Material for Drama Schools*

SHAKESPEARE

CORIOLANUS Act I Scene 1	Caius Marcius (afterwards called Coriolanus)	From "He that will give good words to thee will flatter" To ". . . What's their seeking?"	An extrovert attacks the citizens of Rome with scorn and contempt.
HENRY IV PART I Act I Scene 3	Hotspur	From "My liege, I did deny no prisoners." To "Betwixt my love and your high majesty."	A passionate and fiery young man is defending himself against what he considers to be unjust charges. The speech gives an opportunity to characterise the fop who approaches him on the battlefield.
KING HENRY V Act I Scene 2	Henry	From "We are glad the Dauphin is so pleasant with us;" To "Convey them with safe conduct. Fare you well."	Henry addresses the French Ambassador who has insulted him in a speech of icy anger, gradually building up to a strong emotional climax. An astringent use of consonants is helpful.
HENRY VI PART II Act V Scene 2	Young Clifford	From "Shame and confusion! All is on the rout;" To "Nothing so heavy as these woes of mine."	Young Clifford discovers his father's body on the battlefield in a scene which should have strong dramatic impact. Deeply felt grief must be released.
KING JOHN Act II Scene 1	Bastard	From "Mad world! Mad kings! Mad composition!" To "Gain, be my lord, for I will worship thee."	This forceful character considers the political scene he has just witnessed in a spirit of robust, amused cynicism. The intellectual argument has to be put over with careful pointing of the key words.

KING RICHARD II Act III Scene 2	Richard	From "Discomfortable cousin!" To "Weak men must fall; for heaven still guards the right."	The splendour of the language here mustn't be allowed to swamp the sense. Richard is strongly attacking the traitor Bolingbroke.
MUCH ADO ABOUT NOTHING Act II Scene 1	Benedick	From "O, she misus'd me . . ." To ". . . and perturbation, follows her."	Benedick, smarting from Beatrice's tongue rails against her, but with wit and a sense of comedy.
MEASURE FOR MEASURE Act II Scene 2	Angelo	From "What's this, what's this? Is this her fault or mine?" To "When men were fond, I smil'd and wond'red how."	A speech of troubled self-examination. Changes of pace should help to achieve the illusion of spontaneity as one thought succeeds another.
OTHELLO Act II Scene 1	Iago	From "Come hither. If thou be'st valiant—" To ". . .and the woman hath found him already."	Iago, the Machiavellian villain is feeding poison about Desdemona and Cassio to his dupe, Roderigo. Iago enjoys evil for evil's sake and this relish should appear in the speech.
ROMEO AND JULIET Act V Scene 1	Romeo	From "Is it e'en so? Then I defy you, stars." To ". . . I will hence tonight." THEN From "Well, Juliet, I will lie with thee to-night." To "What ho! Apothecary!"	This speech has the calm of resolved tragedy. The adolescent Romeo has achieved a fatalistic maturity. Although the speech is apparently a description of the apothecary's shop this mood underlies it all.

Speeches for Men: *Suggested Material for Drama Students*

STRAIGHT, SERIOUS SPEECHES

ALBERT'S BRIDGE Tom Stoppard *Faber & Faber* *French, New York*	Albert		From "I shan't wave." To "Don't wave, don't look down—Don't fall."	Albert is painting a big girdered railway bridge. He is describing his job and what he can see below.
CAMINO REAL Tennessee Williams *Penguin*	Lord Byron	Block 8	From "That's very true, senor." To "*Make voyages!* Attempt them! there's nothing else."	Byron tells Casanova that he feels that his poetic talent is dwindling. A big scale speech demanding a sense of style in voice and movement. Note that his limp is very slight. No Richard III effects should be tried!
THE GLASS MENAGERIE Tennessee Williams *Penguin*	Tom	Scene 7	From "I didn't go to the moon." To "And so goodbye."	Tom is thinking about his sister Laura in a tenderly nostalgic speech. It should not be hurried.
THE HOMECOMING Harold Pinter *Eyre-Methuen* *French, New York*	Lenny	Act I	From "One night, not too long ago" To ". . . and a couple of turns of the boot and sort of left it at that."	He is telling his sister-in-law, in a kind of verbal flirtation of a probably made-up incident. However it must be put over with apparent conviction. A North London accent is appropriate.

KRAPP'S LAST TAPE Samuel Beckett *Faber & Faber* *French, New York*	Krapp		From "Spiritually a year of profound gloom and indigence . . ." To ". . . up and down, and from side to side." THEN "Just been listening to that stupid bastard I took myself for thirty years ago!"	A difficult but rewarding speech. The old man Krapp is listening to his voice as a young man on a tape. This could be done with his back to the audience with the actor speaking the 'taped' words. At the end he turns and speaks the last words as himself in old age.
LONG DAY'S JOURNEY INTO NIGHT Eugene O'Neill *Jonathan Cape* *Yale University Press*	Edmund	Act VI	From "You've just told me some high spots in your memories. Want to hear mine?" To ". . . who must always be a little in love with death."	The words should be spoken in a drunk, defensively maudlin manner, but the self-pity should not be overdone. A great deal of vocal modulation is required.
NEXT TIME I'LL SING TO YOU James Saunders *André Deutsch*	Rudge		From "There is the hut, unseen in the darkness . . ." To "The Hermit is dead."	A useful, short, but quietly effective speech which could be put in contrast to a more extrovert one. Rudge, a young man is creating the atmosphere in which the Hermit is slowly dying. Sensitivity is called for.
THE REAL THING Tom Stoppard *Methuen*	Henry	Act II Scene 5	From "This thing here . . ." To ". . .oo, oo—ouch!"	A typically witty Stoppard speech. The playwright's own consuming passion for his craft underlies the apparently conversational description of the making of a cricket bat. His character, Henry, is also a playwright. The two levels in the speech have to be conveyed by the actor.

ROSENCRANTZ AND GUILDENSTERN ARE DEAD Tom Stoppard *French*	Rosencrantz	Act II	From "It could go on for ever . . ." To "They wouldn't come."	A series of verbal acrobatics, calling for a quick, light touch and a sense of timing. The comedy must not be forced.
THE TYPISTS Murray Schisgal *Dramatists Play Service Inc*	Paul		From "I was born in a poor section of Brooklyn." To ". . . it's as if you were born two steps behind the next fellow."	Paul is a twenty year old typist in an office. He is remembering his childhood in an unhappy home, and a traumatic, formative incident during his adolescence. A speech of emotional recall which should not be sentimentalised.

Speeches for Men: *Suggested Material for Drama Students*

COMEDY

ABSURD PERSON SINGULAR Alan Ayckbourn *French*	Geoffrey	Act II	From "You all right? You're still in your dressing-gown, did you know?" To "What I lack in morals—I make up in ethics."	Geoffrey is good-looking, confident and easy-going. A conversational style is needed but with plenty of comedy pace and attack.
THE CRITIC R. B. Sheridan *Oxford Paperbacks* *Hill and Wang* *(in 6 plays ed.* *Kierenberger)*	Mr Puff		From "Hark'ee—by advertisements—" To "—and so, sir, you have my history."	The character is the author of a play that is to be rehearsed. He is here describing his methods of advertising in order to draw money from a gullible public. This is a bravura role demanding a feeling for late eighteenth century style in movement and the use of the voice. His affectation should not be exaggerated.
DESIGN FOR LIVING Noel Coward *French*	Otto	Act I	From "Well, one thing that magnificent outburst has done for me . . ." To "I wish you were dead and in hell!"	Otto is a painter and is living with Gilda who has been unfaithful to him with their mutual friend Leo. He returns unexpectedly to find the two of them laughing helplessly. A technically difficult speech calling for explosive energy, neat articulation and varied modulation of pitch.

53

FILUMENA Eduardo de Filippo *French*	Domenico	Act III	From "Have I made you happy, Filumena?" To "... I swear that I'll still marry you."	The middle-aged Domenico is entreating his former mistress to tell him which of her three sons is his. A volatile, Italianate style is needed with plenty of gesture and a broken accent.
HADRIAN VII Peter Luke *French*	Rolfe	Act I	From "Bless me, Father, for I have sinned." To "... pray, for me to the Lord our God."	Rolfe, an eccentric is making a most unconventional confession. The ritual part at the beginning and end should be taken fast. His is an agile mind and great verve accompanies all he says.
LAST OF THE RED HOT LOVERS Neil Simon *Avon (USA)*	Barney	Act III	From "All right, all right, we're all no good." To "Come here, Jeanette."	Barney is middle-aged and in this speech he gives the male point of view with some vehemence. A warmly human character. The play is set in New York.
NO MAN'S LAND Harold Pinter *Eyre-Methuen*	Foster	Act I	From "I must clean the house." To "The right niche, the right happiness."	He is in his thirties and looks after Hirst. The best thing to do in this speech is to let Pinter's rhythms carry you. There are none of the famous Pinter pauses in it. The apparently conversation style is in contrast to the vivid use of language.
THE NORMAN CONQUESTS (TABLE MANNERS) Alan Ayckbourn *Chatto & Windus* *Penguin* *French, New York*	Norman	Act I	From "Oh, well. It's a bit quieter without those two." To "A gigolo trapped in a haystack."	Norman is confiding to Reg his frustration with Annie and his wife, Ruth. He is full of grievances and the effect is one of wistfulness mixed with comic ruefulness.

54

THE PHILANTHROPIST Christopher Hampton *French*	Philip	Act II Scene 2	From "I don't know. I've always been a failure with women." To "I adored her."	A wrily humorous account of a first experience of a sexual advance. He is not aware that he is being funny.
THE RULING CLASS Peter Barnes *Heinemann*	Earl of Gurney	Scene 4	From "Deformed, unfinished, sent before me time . . ." To "One sidled up to Jack, then there were five."	The character is paranoid and schizophrenic. In this speech he is, by turns, an actor of the old school playing Richard III, God and Jack the Ripper. The whole speech should be taken apparently seriously, but invested with a sardonic zest. A big-scale style of acting is necessary.

Speeches for Men: *Suggested Material for Drama Students*

CHARACTER

AMADEUS Peter Shaffer *Penguin*	Salieri	Act I	From "Capisco . . . I know my fate . . ." To ". . . if not to teach God his lesson."	A key speech from the play. Salieri pours out his bitterness as he realises that God has given him the perception to recognize genius—but only a second-rate talent.
DUET FOR ONE Tom Kempinski *French*	Dr Feldmann	Act II Session 5	From "Don't play silly buggers with me, Miss Abrahams . . ." To ". . . get off your arse and fight!"	Feldmann is a typical German psychiatrist—experienced and caring deeply for his patients. This has to be spoken in a hiss of seemingly genuine, quiet anger.
EQUUS Peter Shaffer *French*	Dysart	Act II Last Scene	From "All right, I'll take it away . . ." To ". . . and it never comes out."	The psychiatrist who has been treating Alan reflects bitterly on Alan's probable future in a materialistic world and on the nature of his own work "standing in the dark with a pick in my hand—picking at heads".
FORTY YEARS ON Alan Bennett *Faber & Faber* *French, New York*	Headmaster	Act I	From "This school, this Albion House . . ." To ". . . and the play will begin shortly."	This is the Headmaster's last term. He addresses the boys in a nicely judged mixture of satire and comedy. A light, firm touch, astringent use of consonants and a brisk pace are required.
THE HOMECOMING Harold Pinter *Eyre-Methuen*	Max	Act I	From "He talks to me about horses." To "And he talks to me about horses."	A short but richly evocative speech from the elderly Cockney Max, calling for tremendous zest and an enjoyment of language.

56

Title / Author / Publisher	Character	Act	Extract	Notes
A MAN FOR ALL SEASONS Robert Bolt *Heinemann* *French, New York*	Sir Thomas More	Act II	From "My Lord! My lord, when I was practising the law," To "—but because I would not bend to the marriage."	More's last speech at his trial. He speaks now only consulting his own interests, quietly but from passionate conviction. His body has been wasted by prison, but his spirit illuminates all that he is saying.
SALOMÉ Oscar Wilde *Penguin*	Herod		From "Listen. I have jewels hidden in this place." To "I will give thee the veil of the sanctuary."	A seductive speech made to Salomé by Herod, Tetrarch of Judaea. Restraint is vital in this 'purple passage'; otherwise it may become laughably melodramatic.
SEMI DETACHED David Turner *Evans*	Fred	Act I	From "I'm getting a bit cheesed with your basic elementary pubescence." To "And very homely, warm and—reassuring it is, too."	A short, pungent piece of satire. A middle-aged suburban father, an insurance agent, talks to his son about the different makes of motor in a self-consciously 'posh' accent of no particular region. A savagely comic speech.
SLEUTH Anthony Shaffer *French*	Andrew	Act I	From "Since you appear to know so much . . ." To ". . . as neat and as gaudy as ever he was."	Andrew, a fleshy, gone to seed detective story writer is reading what he has just typed. The speech satirises the typical dénouement of the genre. It calls for sophisticated polish and a firm, keenly-pointed attack.
THE UNION OFFICIAL George Melly (Mixed Doubles) *Methuen*	Union Official		From "Totally unacceptable!" To "you know where to find me."	A highly amusing monologue in which a hectoring Union Official at a meeting with his bosses is gradually worn down and embarrassed by a series of telephone conversations with his domineering wife. It will only be funny if the actor appears to be suffering genuine embarrassment.

Speeches for Men: *Suggested Material for Drama Students*

SHAKESPEARE

KING HENRY V Act IV Scene 1	Henry	From "Upon the King! Let us our lives, our souls," To "Sleeps in Elysium;"	The disguised king is wandering among his sleeping army the night before Agincourt. A grave, philosophical speech about the responsibilities of king-ship. He envies the peaceful sleep of his subjects.
HENRY VI PART III Act I Scene 4	York	From "She-wolf of France, but worse than wolves of France." To "'Gainst thee, fell Clifford, and thee, false Frenchwoman."	York, standing on a hillock and wearing a paper crown has been taunted by Margaret with the death of his son Rutland. This is his reply to her—firm and dignified. At the end, however, he sheds tears for his dead boy.
KING HENRY VI PART III Act II Scene 5	Son	From "Ill blows the wind that profits nobody." To "And no more words till they have flow'd their fill."	As he starts to search the man whom he has killed, for crowns, the son discovers that it is his father. The speech calls for the release of depths of emotion.
THE MERRY WIVES OF WINDSOR Act II Scene 2	Ford	From "What a damn'd Epicurean rascal is this!" To "Fie, fie, fie! cuckold! cuckold! cuckold!"	A prose speech which has to be delivered with intensity and passion. Ford is eaten up with jealousy to a laughable degree.
MUCH ADO ABOUT NOTHING Act II Scene 3	Benedick	From "I do much wonder . . ." To "I will hide me in the arbour."	The confirmed bachelor Benedick contemplates the pitiable state of Claudio who has fallen in love. Then he considers if such a fate could befall him. The prose is rhythmical and the approach needs to be light and witty.

58

RICHARD II Act III Scene 3	Richard	From "What must the King do now? Must he submit?" To "For night-owls shriek where mounting larks should sing."	A speech of strong contrasts of moods, ranging from poetic fancy to self pity. Careful modulation of voice amount is needed as Richard is speaking some of the speech from the castle walls to Northumberland in the court below.
ROMEO AND JULIET Act V Scene 3	Romeo	From "How oft when men are at the point of death" To "Thy drugs are quick. Thus with a kiss I die."	Romeo finds the supposedly dead Juliet in the tomb of the Capulets. A speech of powerful emotion, lyrically expressed with such evocative imagery that Shakespeare does much of the work for the actor, provided that his heart and mind are behind the words.
THE TAMING OF THE SHREW Act IV Scene 1	Petruchio	From "Thus have I politicly begun my reign," To "Now let him speak; 'tis charity to show."	Petruchio is relishing his role as the tamer of Katharina. It has to be put over with gusto but also with some charm, otherwise he appears merely a boorish bully.
TROILUS AND CRESSIDA Act I Scene 3	Ulysses	From "The heavens themselves, the planets, and this centre," To "And the rude son should strike his father dead;"	This is part of a long speech of grave beauty in which Shakespeare sets out his creed. A speech which will repay thoughtful study.
THE WINTER'S TALE Act IV Scene 4	Autolycus	From "Ha, ha! what a fool Honesty is!" To ". . . I had not left a purse alive in the whole army."	Autolycus is a rogue, but an engaging one. Here he is exulting in his skill at picking the pockets of the gullible public.

Men and Women: *Suggested Material for Children's Theatre*

ALAN AND THE KING'S DAUGHTERS Helen Murdoch *French*	Winnie	Act I Scene 1	From "Now, the next thing is to mix the dry ingredients, and the spell's complete."
BEAUTY AND THE BEAST Ted Hughes *Faber & Faber*	Floreat		From "Why are you keeping me in this cave?" To "I must stop them. Come back."
CHARLIE AND THE CHOCOLATE FACTORY Roald Dahl (ad R. George) *Puffin Books*	Narrator	Scene 1	From "Welcome to the tale of a delicious adventure in a wonderful land." To "Where are you, Augustus Gloop?"
THE COMING OF THE KINGS Ted Hughes *Faber & Faber*	Minstrel		From "I've just had an astounding dream . . ." To "Because I dare not look. Inside the shed."
FANNY'S FIRST PLAY George Bernard Shaw *Heinemann* *French, New York*	Margaret Knox	Prologue	From "We're going to act a play . . ." To "I got so tired of the plays . . ." THEN From "But when I hinted at it to the manager . . ." To "Just write a play and act in it yourself."

THE HAPPY PRINCE Oscar Wilde *Duckworth*	Narrator		From "High above the city, on a tall column, stood the statue of the Happy Prince." To "... for he did not approve of children dreaming."
THE HEARTLESS PRINCESS Franklyn Black *French*	Fox	Act I Scene 1	From "It's no use you rumblin' and grumblin' like that!" To "... anyone'ud think they're 'untin mice, instead of a fox! Blimey!"
THE INSECT PLAY The Brothers Čapek *Oxford Paperbacks* *French, New York*	Tramp	Prologue	From "'ello. What yer doin'? ketchin' butterflies?" To "It's worth while learnin' what it's all about." (Omit Lepidopterist's lines.)
KING CAT David Grant *Longman*	Catlin		From "Dark? It was a lovely bright night" To "That's enough for now. No, no more!"
OLIVER TWIST Charles Dickens (ad Brian Way) *Pitman*	Noah Claypole		From "They've got Sikes." To "... whilst from the crowd there came a tremendous cheer ..."
THE OWL AND THE PUSSY CAT WENT TO SEE Sheila Ruskin and David Wood *French*	Plum Pudding Flea		From "Ha, ha, ha, ha. I saw them going off, oh yes I did." To "... and use her to eat all the others with ... ha, ha, ha ..."

PETER PAN J. M. Barrie *Hodder and Stoughton* *French, New York*	Peter	Act IV	From "Who is that?" To "And now to rescue Wendy."
THE MYSTERY OF THE PIE AND THE PATTY-PAN Beatrix Potter (dram. Rona Laurie) *Frederick Warne*	Duchess		From "A letter for me? Thank you, Postman." To "Why shouldn't I rush along and put my pie into Ribby's oven when Ribby isn't there?"
THE SEA KING'S DAUGHTER Margaret Harding *French*	Serpent		From "It's useless to cry out for help now," To ". . .or I shall not be so gentle with you." (Omit Marina's lines)
SEAN, THE FOOL, THE DEVIL AND THE CATS Ted Hughes *Faber & Faber*	The Fool		From "Sean follows the cat." To "A strange huge cat."
THE SELFISH GIANT Oscar Wilde *Duckworth*	Narrator		From "Every afternoon, as they were coming home from school, the children used to go and play in the Giant's garden." To "He was a very selfish Giant."
THE SNOW QUEEN Hans Andersen (ad Magito and Weil) *Heinemann* *French, New York*	Storyteller		From "Ah! She's snoring now!" To "I'll light the lamp."

THERE WAS AN OLD WOMAN David Wood *French*	The Great Boon	Prologue	From "And now, may I kindly beg, borrow or steal two young members of the audience?" To "May I change places with the Witch!"
THE TINDER BOX Nicholas Stuart Gray *Oxford University Press* *French, New York*	Witch		From "She doesn't like me. Odd little thing!" To "I told you to be quiet!"
TOAD OF TOAD HALL A. A. Milne (ad Kenneth Grahame) *French*	Toad		From "I'll wear the light brown suit." To "The good Rat will chuckle when I tell him."

It's important to read the whole play, once you have chosen your speech

ONLY by doing this will you be able to give an in-depth performance of the character. Avoid long, introductory explanations of the plot and setting. Usually the panel of judges know the play. They are also working to a tight schedule and want to see you in action without delay.

It is vital to keep to any stipulated times for the speeches. Some of the ones suggested in this book may over-run those times and may need to be curtailed.

On the day of the audition

1. Get there early, but not too early.

2. Try not to let the nervousness of other people who are waiting affect you.

3. Don't worry if everyone else in the room appears to have greater experience than you have.

4. Wear clothes that are helpful and that you can move **easily** in. Very tight jeans or skirts and exaggeratedly high h**eels are** not a good idea for the girls, for example.

5. Once you start acting, sink yourself in the charac**ter and** situation and try to forget the artificiality of the occasion.

I hope that you will enjoy the search for suitable materi**al and** that when the day of the audition arrives, you will fe**el that** at least you have given yourself the best possible cha**nce of** success.